CW00863964

looking for summer
by
gurpreet raulia

for those who are
becoming

acknowledgements

there are many people who made this dream possible for me. my mother, for nurturing me and showing me love to bring me here. my brother and sister for presumably teaching me english, couldn't be here without you both. my beautiful soul sisters in canada for giving me confidence and endless support in all my hopes and dreams. to all the other family members who have had faith in me. to everyone who's invested in me, even if it's a dreamcatcher from the dollar store. to the friends that i am so lucky to have and who support everything i do. and also, thanks to everyone to inspired my poetry. where would i be if it wasn't for all of those people and experiences? thank you to everyone for making this happen.

a note on the text from the i

before i get into semantics, i want to speak to you in my plainest english. i don't know what this book will make you feel. however, i am excited for you to have a journey with me. these words you will read have come from a really special part of my heart. they've come from feelings of happiness, spirituality, sadness, inspiration, depression, anxiety, love but most of all: honesty. these are my truths. the truths of my heart, my mind but most importantly, of my soul. i can only wish that these words will inspire you or make you feel anything; it would be an honour. but what i want is for you to build a relationship with my words. it needs not to be a good relationship. but i want for you to connect. of course i cannot force this, but i have tried to achieve this. sometimes in life we need honesty. it may not be clear in what form we receive it. it may not be clear what the honesty addresses. but i feel it is important that we always have somebody's truth. as guidance. as inspiration. as hope.

these words have probably helped me through a hard time. i have built a personal relationship with these words. and now i am sharing them with you. it's scary. sharing a part of your heart, mind and soul amongst others. but it's important to do it. perhaps you will understand. perhaps you will relate. you do not have to feel intimidated, patronised or scared by the truth. the truth can be uplifting and simply refreshing. i have tried to squeeze my abundant thoughts into these poems. and these poems come in different sizes and forms. being a producer of words does not necessarily mean i can always understand them. it's not easy write down feelings and thoughts that words have never before explained. so please, be understanding and be thoughtful. make the words your own. go on a journey with me and the words, a journey to summer. have a good trip.

-gurpreet

for you: a playlist for when you read these poems
(in no specific order)

nights- frank ocean
merry christmas mr. lawrence- ryuichi sakamoto
selling flowers- slow hollows
that easy- yellow days
human nature- michael jackson
the way life goes- lil uzi vert, oh wonder
drew barrymore- sza
you there- aquilo
rideaux lunaires- chilly gonzales
show me how- men i trust
finesse- drake
self control- frank ocean
she's mine pt.2- j.cole
hero- regina spektor
nothing's going to keep me down- yellow days
tonya- brockhampton
higgs- frank ocean
summer- the carters
poetic justice- kendrick lamar, drake
you- sebastian roca
yosemite- travis scott
love galore- sza, travis scott
after the storm- kali uchis, tyler the creator and
bootsy collins
white ferrari- frank ocean

afterglow- wilkinson, becky hill
marvins room- drake
everytime- boy pablo
i wonder- kanye west
the way things change- yellow days
i love you so- the walters
seigfried- frank ocean
drowsy- banes world
same drugs- chance the rapper
easily- bruno major
best part- daniel caesar, h.e.r.
moodna, once with grace- gus dapperton
bad religion- frank ocean
holding on- yellow days
hello stranger- barbara lewis
visions of gideon- sufjan stevens
lost boy- jaden smith
israel- willow
so many details- toro y moi
lover's carvings- bibio
from eden- hozier
get you- daniel caesar
islands- young the giant
everybody wants to rule the world- tears for fears
all is now harmed- ben howard
4422- drake, sampha
chanel- frank ocean
january 28th- j. cole

contents

sub-zero

i am looking for summer,
these grey skies are overbearing
warning: skin may show signs of wearing

i am looking for summer,
but my eyes are blank
sinking in the well of an oxygen tank

i am looking for summer,
i am tired of winter
and i simply want to feel warm
(even if i'm really not)

we yearn for distance
and then wallow in the pain
of being alone

the earth tears herself like paper
she tries to rid herself of the stories
she hates to carry
on her back
she's tired of the damage
so she destroys herself

do i not know if this is love
because it isn't
or because i have never
been in it
to know

i feel that i am at times
too romantic
so much so that i confuse
puppy love for thriving romance
but more than confusing
and ruining myself i forget,
that i string along the other
like a kitten with yarn
aimlessly creating a mess
that i have no energy in me
to clean up

there's a numbness
it is strung like a harp
but there's no sound
there's no beauty in it
and there's no pain in it
it's white with no feeling

i fumble attempting
my own mother tongue
i untrained myself through shame
ignorant
to the idea of how hard it would be
to train myself yet again
my muscle memory is off

it hurts me
that someone so good
can be so hurt
and the vicious cycle
laughs in joy
with a smug sneer,
that it has two new victims

there are bridges now
and borders
that i set fire to
the ashes lay all over my body
and they make me choke
since i am sooted with regret

i lay and argue with my sleepless body
lapping in and out of consciousness
and awareness of myself
questioning everything i want
and everything i am
in the end i vow to put myself first
my own biggest priority
yet i torture myself to make sure
that what i'm doing is the right thing

i let you consume me
like a bowl of soup with all the good bits
and i let you spit me out with full force
i let you mop me up and say sorry
i was your object and your tool
and i will never be that ever again

how will i know that i have
healed
when the only signals that
i've been given are painful,
who will teach me recovery

why use tear gas
if we're crying anyway
clothes we can't fit in
homes we can't live in
skin we can't breathe in
we are crying anyway

i tried to remove the emptiness
by making myself empty
i tried to fight the mental
with the physical
but i forgot to love both,
or either of them,
and i left myself crippled by war

you spoilt me with so much
hurt
it felt selfish to ask for some
love
for once

my mind strung along you
and my heart searched elsewhere
i created a distance so vast
and got lost in between
balancing act on this tightrope
that i've made

the sun kissed me in ways
that others will envy
so they mock me
before laying into a sunbed
'shade four please'
when did my culture become
a number

my mother abandoned wearing
her salwar and kameez on the streets,
and limited her culture to jeans and a top,
she asks me everyday if she is looking okay,
as she was not allowed for her two cultures
to coexist, by people who may laugh
or look at her differently
for being who she is

i was brought roses
and they were handed to me
to be taken by the thorns

though i have not a bad word to say
that you could not understand my pain
i have nothing but emptiness
towards that year or so of numbness
the year or so that disappeared
that i cannot understand anymore

i am a cup overflowing
with water and you're a tap
and nobody is turning you off
i scream in the oceans i'm afraid of
i could never learn to swim

i put so many locks
on myself, in my interior,
that i don't know which key is for
which lock. and now i can never
let anyone in

gurpreet raulia

we instilled a word
within our language
to signal when we don't want
something to happen but we
forgot
we neglected, instilling it into
some of our minds
so some continue to ignore it

you chose carpets i didn't like,
painted the walls in the colour that
reminded me of the darkness in my mind,
and there were dead flowers on the table,
you made a home out of me and got
too comfortable, using up my energy but
paying no bills.

there is nothing more tiring
than doing nothing
and then there is nothing
to fix and nothing to improve
why do you think you haven't
moved in three days

smashed glass
you cut me, but you catch the
sun
prisms of light
your aura so endearing,
    damaging

my fingertips twitch with the feeling of the
unknown as i crumble the soil between
my senses,
heavens above stumble
i separate myself from this land and its
history as it covers
my melanin infused skin
with racist dirt

for india, i am too english,
for england, i'm too ethnic,
and i am left so challenged,
war tattooed onto my
diasporic identity,
trying to find balance within
my troubled entity.

i only taught myself to feel raw
etching through myself
in order to feel alive
but i killed myself with every trauma
you can't save a dead thing

-can you?

you know too much
about the world
so many things your mind
deserves so much better than
to be exposed to,
your sweet mind,
i wish i could kiss it
inside and out and wipe away
the dust

you gave me love in
so much abundance
that it's as if i'd been given
a credit card and i was a spoilt child
who had never known
such affection nor attention
but i left you broke
and broken

i am always an ocean, there is always saltwater
streaming from my eyes and stinging
i am always malleable and
always misshapen and always falling over
niagara i am always falling
i am always falling always
fal
l
ing
you opened your umbrella
to shelter yourself from me
but don't worry i'll catch myself
even puddles rise again

i can't hear the songs the same again
you took all the notes with you
left them with no rhythm
you muted them to my senses
you took my music away

what i did not get from childhood
i sought in you and your own,
what i could never understand
the privilege,
i was envious of it i was sad,
that i never had the nuclear family unit
just a nuclear reaction,
played out in the shape of a family

you are torture
disguised in hurt

what do you do when two parts of
yourself are at war amongst you,
what do you do when it's your people
killing your people,
how do you seek revenge for something
within you?

drought in my skin
i am clay, a masterpiece
crumbling, forever
being varnished to hide
all my endeavours
to break out of this shell
drying deep within
climbing out of cupboards
to find the sun
drought will never win

the poetry hangs off my tongue
there are so many thoughts
i want to translate
but there aren't words that
know me
well enough to embrace my
ideas
and make sense of what
i want you all to know

you saw in me nothing except
exactly what you wanted
so i spent the next few days
ridding myself of that feeling
forgetting your drive
detoxing the room
of your scent, of your essence,
of your hunger,
to use me to make yourself
feel empowered

my temperament is
as exhausting as a two year old
you are my world
for maybe a week or two
and then my inner dramatist
attempts to write a new story
for myself, a new twist
that nobody saw coming
and suddenly you are no longer my
absolute world, rather just
an illusion, a dimension of the world
that i am now tired of
and now want to explore a new one

-plot twist

how can you be a part of a community
when you are trying to govern it
to your selfish needs
and in doing so
ripping it a pa r t

there are so many people within me
they all want different things
but i am running races with different
versions of myself
and sometimes i can't keep up

what's the human cost from this
paradise lost
we are left drawing our own margins,
our everwatching eyes
finding ourselves by the seaside
eroding with the coast

each wave of your supernatural entity
washes and leaves me empty
i can't swim but i couldn't bear to drown
forever trying to find signal
in your english channels

you wanted to pawn me in
in return for something better
because you knew how valuable i was
yet your greed made you want
so much more

if you are a man of this house
you will not be a force within it
and force the people of it
to be who you want them to be

you've drank the blood of us all
and drained us emotionally,
mentally

if you are a man of this house
you will relinquish power
you will let us live as opposed
to just being life

there is nothing sadder
than when your faith becomes
the reason for your pitfall
because something that brings you peace
should never be the reason you fall
at the hands of another

so the screams, the torture, the sheer
atrocity to the Sikhs, operation blue star
the Jews, the holocaust
the Syrians, 'protection of the people',
we are senseless and desensitised

their souls rest now
though that's how they should have been
when they were alive.

you walked into my life
as if i was a coffee shop
you paid for my love
but asked for the petty change back

they say eating celery
burns more calories than it has
was i your celery?
because you feel better
and i am gone

don't you miss when we wished together
had the same dreams together
slept sweetly together
breathed together
now the only thing we have
together
is this distance
we don't even smoke the same anymore
or laugh at the same jokes
we don't know each other anymore
time is so fast
and we don't chase it together

i've become dumb with loss
i can't say your name anymore
and you were all i ever knew

to me you were a smartphone,
lost touch with the world
busy with my touch screen,
became anti-social as you became
my social media
you were my society
but you drained my battery life
and provided me no charger
needed recharging
still feeling empty

you act like a lion
your head beaming
with pride but really
you're a housecat
craving for attention

what's the use in being
beautiful

why do you crave to be
perfect

what's the perfection in
having no flaws

what's the need to
pretend

we try so hard to be plastic
but get choked by it
looped around our necks

we get choked by our own
dead wishes

we really need to look after
each one another

she made my heart feel so
lucky to have known a girl
like her but i knew it was
something so much more
special than liking her face
i just felt so stupid
for trying to trace her line
around my circle

the warmth of the sun hugs me
there is so much strength in nature
become one with it
become power

there is so much pressure
to fill these pages
leaving no white spaces
a metaphor for life in these words
but the white spaces say
so much more than the words at times
what i don't have, what i leave out
will tell more than what i can say
the whiteness outdoes the ink
it soaks it up and spits it out
onto your hands whilst you
flip through these pages
your hands picking up the whiteness
and the stories that i could not tell

a man who has no truth within him
no goodness in his soul
will use his aggression and his force
to make up for the cold space
the universe left in his heart
the starvation the universe gave
his undeserving nature
and he will be saddened by the injustice
not knowing that all he must do
is earn the key that will give him
real happiness and truth

of course i am okay
but i'm melting within
i look okay but how
do i explain, mrs doctor,
that i am always just okay
my okay, my mode, my average
is always crumbling
of course i'm fine if i've become used to
feeling this melancholy
feeling this slow hollow

don't ask why i'm crying
why i cannot breathe or why
my chest is unable to stay
calm and serene or why my fingers
feel like they're numbing
if i knew don't you think i would
stop it already don't you think
i would be fine and i wouldn't
stop myself from breaking down because
there's too many notifications
on my phone or too many
people on the roads or i left my
purse at home but i'm already in
the queue don't you think
i would stop this feeling

you can call it an irrational fear
'why would you be letting
your mind be consumed by
these thoughts if you do not know of
its truth' but don't forget
the mind manifests its own truths sometimes
and there is no truth scarier to me
than the idea that i will not
be able to bear
oh the fear that i will not bear
an angel or two of my likeness
that there will not be someone
to call me their mother
i am so afraid

daydreamer, you floater,
what is the end game
where are you heading,
away from me? constantly
running away from me
knowing full well that you
are running from what you
want to see of yourself
within me but just weren't
ready to accept

two years of waste,
impulsive satisfaction
temporary feeling
you were just empty calories
eating and eating at
causing more damage than
sham happiness

nowadays we just sleep
with our pillows
and we never wash them
desperate to hold onto memories
that will only make us sick

the day you let me back
into your bed is the day
i let you back into my head

communication is so
easily manipulated
it makes no difference to
vow to be clear
there's no limit on
being a good liar

you reduce women to their
body parts, thinking you're
greater but acting nothing
short of a dick

i wish i could raise you up,
earth and humanity,
like my child birthed by love,
i wish i could see you grow
and fly like a dove but
the world is bitter and though i never liked coffee
i liked the way you made it
but this time, mister,
god knows, you're no barista,
since now our skies are falling
our children like always
are hated for their skin and there are really people
making thrones, hiding sins, placing crowns
on their own heads, thinking they is pure for the
way they is bred,
still they don't pick up white bread
for good health they yearn,
so they pick up the wholemeal, brown bread,
yet look at my brown skin with disdain
my mother tongue bringing them pain
as if my mother can't cook what they eat
or speak what they speak,
or as if i don't sit in a classroom,
paying thousands i don't own,
sitting in my brown skin all on my own,

reading white stories, white narrative, white history,
so much so that i know not
of my history, know not
of my heritage,
so white-washed that i'm ecstatic
that some strange ancestry informatics
told me that my great-great-great grandfather
was baptised in norway, a european region,
and like that, i break my allegion
with my skin, with my faith
the white poison told me once to my face
that i had to change my name if i were to date
stripped me of my culture just because he didn't rate
who i are?
i am sickened that even i esteemed the whiteness
more than,
my roasted oatmeal and raisin bran,
so i sit in tears in the fear of my colour
searching for a deed poll to change my name
sitting there, blasphemy, leaving my parents to
blame,
these words, pure, they're injected with melanin
so before you lay in that deathbed think of this
poem i've written from my sadness within,
that we have had to question our identity

paint over our ethnicities
with brushes made by our own people,
just so i can feel more validated by those
who will spite me regardless
all because the sun held me
for a little bit longer before throwing me
onto a planet that is burning anyway,
a world where colour is hated
though it's pigment concentrated
and a cheeto in a wig cheats the law
so that our trans brothers and sisters are buried so
under a veil of what we should be
this is a halloween who's end we'll never see,
our families in the middle east being broken by
war,
tell me, dear earth, what else is in store,
Orlando, Parkland, say their names,
air pollution, climate change, hurricanes,
the refugees, Palestine, say their names,
our world is crashing down now,
by guns and evil people
by a hatred of humanity
we can't even talk about race
because someone always thinks they're winning,
you don't need to be religious to see the extent of
this sinning,

i can't tell you the end from the beginning,
or what else our universe is bringing,
but know that i am sad,
you should be too,
and maybe then, we'll find a way through.

-what we should be

lukewarm

i fall in love so easily
with noises with sounds, with faces
so how do i know what true 'love' is,
i will just have to continue to
appreciate everything i can
until i feel that special thing
they talk about in jazz songs
the thing everyone knows but me

i crave the ocean
though i cannot swim
i crave the waves
though i will not survive
i crave the sound
because i can feel

i sit and untangle my wires
i try my best to fix this mess
catching people in the web
and slowly looping them out

we exist in different time zones
we speak in different dialects,
in different accents
yet we communicate with
the same hurt in
different traumas through
different experiences
all in the same sadness
still in the same strength

i will offer all i can,
just two cents of
broken knowledge
but one million pounds
worth of heart ache
to guide you through

i cry in bed
screaming squirming
wishing i was not
born with the extra x
but this monthly pain
is a reasonable price to pay
to prove to the world that
being a girl is not a shortcoming
of mine

there are lines we try to erase
some by taking lines
but we cry and try to draw over them
knowing it'll never be perfect
can't perfect what was there, before,
so we retrace everlong
waiting for a new flame
to reignite itself
wait for the sparks

i want the skies to cry
and cleanse me with its upset
i hope to make it smile

i could never create
a new version of myself
but i have remodelled
recovered with papier-mâché
waiting to dry and become hardened
into one confident shape

"send yourself back to the darkness"
"send yourself back to the darkness"
the darkness continues to talk
about itself within my head
in the third person
it's obnoxious but has a magnetic pull
i'm here again but i don't want to be
but the fire within me
provides me light
within the darkness, i find sight

i will never harbour hatred
the way i did for you
i will release it with all my power
and free myself of negativity
a cynic shower
i cannot dwell on a past like the one you
dared subject me to

the truth is what we are encouraged to tell
it's the hardest thing to face
the most difficult thing to grasp
and the most painful thing to hear
but always the most empowering thing to
know

i am sick of the sun and rain
fighting each other
when they create such beautiful things
if rainbows were forever
maybe we'd have world peace
maybe if we'd coexist for once
maybe we'd see how good
can eliminate the bad
becoming one in the monsoon

it's been three weeks
since you went to church
what god are you praying to now
who's answering your prayers
is it a lover who loves poems about cigarettes
more than you, leaving your hair
smelling like tobacco?
i hope not,
he won't love you like you should be loved
rise from his ashes

i never wanted to tell you
i couldn't do it anymore
'the universe will bring
what you want
when you're truly ready
to receive it'
she lifted my chin, tucked hair
behind my ear before
i told you,
after my heart made me think
i have every reason to fall in love

the walls closed in on me
my hands couldn't bear that kind
of pressure but i refuse to let
anyone bear it for me
so i pushed back with all my might
protecting myself from collapse

gurpreet raulia

your words know how
to pull the strings that release
the tears from my eyes
and the butterflies from my lungs

the universe plucked out your name
from my hurt and my hatred
it has taught me to never be fazed by
you again
i am cleansed from your potion
my body finally belongs to me

the oak doors were so heavy
they trapped the scary outdoors
they enveloped me into a new world
into a safety and it was so calm
i could hear the serenity in the whispers,
in the tapping of the keyboard,
the sound of the coffee machine, ambient,
in the footsteps of families,
the warm light creeping in through the plentiful
windows i felt like i was at home
within my estranged home

darling you are my astrology
you may not be my truth
but you fascinate me
even if others don't believe in you
i'll keep you close to me
we'll become a constellation
if you want to protect me
in such a way, i'll let you guide me

gurpreet raulia

i was a deck of cards
a board of monopoly
a game of uno
you played me so well
and i had no clue(do)

i could not help but feel
subjected to your colour's refusal
to pick my shade, to select my hex code
ruined the colour palette so
you wouldn't create anything with me,
paint brush and pigment
working together,
clearly you're no artist

i wish for long hair days after i shear it off
i rearrange my outfits, five times before i go,
what makes me think i know what i want
who lets me think this is okay,
who am i to know,
what 'okay' is

lost abandoned unsettled
left with these pieces of metal
west pier, full of stories

the last thing i can be is a welder
put up your hands and surrender
to the hopelessness of our love in this
ironically and iconically ionic town,
our ionic love.

it seems that my
couture designer lipstick
has been confused for a
pritt-stick these last
four hundred years
and now i am unsealing
my lips finally peeling
maybe i'll find my voice once again

-find me a beauty guru

i bite the inside of my cheeks
i rip apart my soft parts
i give them to you
i'll leave the hard parts soaking
like almonds overnight
fuelling your brain power over me
ever more

i coat my hair with yoghurt
i drizzle it with honey
i want to feel nourished
in the most natural way,
i endeavour for the effortless

i go to your house
and change all of the clocks
so that we can work on things
at my pace

these are my words
though they may speak to you
they are mine
do with them what you wish
they are mine but
maybe you can cohabit

put my brain in a microwave
for thirty seconds
it'll help ease the content out
that's how mary berry taught me
how to get the most juice out of a lemon
and i drink lemon water every day
ritually
to make myself feel cleansed

after all the crying
all the denial
all the fighting and all the
a n x i e t y
why did i think
you were still home?

i lay in the milk
my skin soaked in the sustenance
i steal from the child but i thank its mother
dearly, i nourish myself in my serenity
the quiet lapping of the milk
in my hands

i will not let anyone barter for me
i am standing in the shop windows of life
with a fixed price and nobody
has yet been able to afford me

we are so lost in these lanes
squeezing ourselves into tiny
lines
single
file
lines
stepping over our own litter

gurpreet raulia

towering higher than i
how can you see all and
nothing at the same time
like God
cowering really
am i

hearts, give me a break
knives, cut me some slack
meditation, i'll show dedication
weights, bring me down to earth

quick, grab the chadara, cover the windows
let no light out instead of
turning out the lights, very simply
Punjab riddled with fear
but refusing to be crippled by it
living life in disguise
but still living strength

-chadara: sheets

you didn't just come to me
and paint over my troubles
you stripped out each one
with wallpaper remover
and revealed the purity
that was begging
to be released from beneath

nameless
faceless
stateless
fateless
shameless
but no less
than the purest
beauty

i've never seen you before
you are the most familiar stranger
you belong here
within me

i picked up the stars from the ground
and began to throw them back
you said save some for the hard times
so we slipped the stars into our pockets
and embraced, hiding in the darkness

feel free to deface
these intricately patterned
shapes, that vow to provide a voice,
to my intricately patterned thoughts,
they may have no names but
they have a lot of identity
but you can make it your own
give these poems your own names
write all over them, around them
draw the flowers and the bees
that exist around them, make them
your own and take from it
what you wish to

gurpreet raulia

my poetry doesn't even hurt anymore
you opened my cupboards
and dusted out the cobwebs
took out my memories and polished them
i can finally confront them and
display them in a glass cabinet
for all the guests to implore on when they visit

oh honey i'm falling into
the sheets i'm living in joy
and not the type daisy pretended
to feel in her sham marriage with tom
but the type nobody in gatsby felt,
but everyone wanted to feel

i fall in love with strangers
every single day
it's about time i stop
using a word like that so loosely
'strangers'

become a teacher of the soul
and become a learner of the mind
become understanding of your
many prophecies
become aware and find yourself
worthy, of recovery from more
than just the surface

i go into the same coffee shop
every day of the year
and each day i go in with a different name
hiding my existence
but bringing light to ones that i do not know
but that i feel others should appreciate
it's strange, of course
but it brings me joy
to pretend to be somebody new
for a day

she is 19, hands and feet adorned
with rich henna, it's infused with
lemon and sugar and eucalyptus
to make it grow darker and imprint stronger
"the darker it is, the more your mother in law
will love you", but never your
heart, darling so be careful,
your name is becoming binded legally
to someone who speaks a language you don't
know, only pieces of, whose heart
speaks in a tone you don't understand
they will never love who you are
they will not know your worth
they will love your womb and what it can do
your hands, still rich with henna, preparing
delicacies you do not know
your worth defined by your uses
but, darling,
you have years waiting for you to jump in
you have an importance that they don't know
be what they cannot understand
use that to your advantage

the night you visited in my dream
there is no denying that i was
feeling, the dictionary definition
of absolutely and terrified,
but i also knew that this feeling
could not be defined by paper
or by science or by history
you had visited me from a
realm that no books can describe
no teacher has explained nor studied
you kept me safe from the
other world, i knew it was special

at times it's not about
getting over things
shutting things away
it's about making peace
with something
and letting it coexist
before it feeds off your
denial and ruins you
from within

where can i buy a cookbook
that will tell me the recipe,
the ingredients and method
that will come to my best use
in order to create the perfect life
but then i realise
that my life is an empty book
and i am the author and the chef
i have to experiment
add and remove different ingredients
and find out the best recipe for
my best life by constantly
working to make it better

how was your today
would you prefer it to
yesterday or, yesteryear?
are you here? looking
for something, do you feel,
okay? how was,
your today?
take care of it,
it has so much to offer.

you do not deserve the
heart break, i will
be right over with my
haberdashery kit, i will,
stitch you up and maybe
add some embellishments

we can drive almost anywhere,
through any hills, any mountains
in any weather, and nothing
is going to change the fact
that we are looking, close to
desperately, for a permanent
destination.

i look at my arms
and i wince in sadness
a feeling that i myself cultivated but
i will not be upset
over something i created
my scars are reminders
of my very progress
what can i do now?
the seeds have been sowed,
now i witness
what i am becoming

your words cut my skin
so sharp though i can curse
you, and hurt you in ways
that will go beyond what
you can physically do to me
i can cast rain on all your days
but i'll just continue
to patch myself up and laugh
as i am numb to your advances
never hurt again

gurpreet raulia

i will work to hold
the key to your heart
and i want you to tell me
when you're ready

i'll turn the key to your
soul and unleash your
mind and open my
eyes to who, what you are

i will swim in your essence
when you're ready
i want to see
what you've birthed of yourself

142

we sat and we cried
as we watched the fireworks
explode after having
told you it couldn't go on
because i needed time for me
the watchers cheered
were they happy for me
or happy to see you
cry for once?

you cannot force creativity
they have tried to protect you
for a reason, wrapping you in
blankets and feeding you bread,
keep yourself warm and let
your mind run free
release your natural beauty

we spend our time
finding what makes us happy
but become tired of it,
separate when you are
exhausted,
but always
reunite with it and
reignite

i held her hand with
all the love my heart could offer
and i let the air encapsulate us
we were thriving off of nature
and i told her i love her
and she laughed
there was so much happiness
in our beings,
i pretended that i didn't know,
that we could never be.

channel that effort
you put into finding love
in others
in yourself

i hope to reincarnate one day
as your mother, or maybe
as your lover so i can guide in you
what you never received

supernatural.
super natural.

gurpreet raulia

this is for those times when
everything feels heavy
this is the crane
lifting your load
letting you catch your breath
this poem is an escape
i hope i can help you.

if you let me in and open
your door i can make you feel
like the only person on this
planet i will be your
release, do you think
you could just unlock the door
can you let me find my way
to you

the goosebumps are so immense
when i hear those songs
that remind me of you
my body knows my memories
better than my mind does

you dipped fingers into
my mind and mixed it
into your tea,
drinking me in all essence like
a potion, knowing me
inside and out

gurpreet raulia

you are the dream i have
the steam from my tea, your
coffee (that you're only drinking
because you don't want to
waste the bag you accidentally
bought), our eyes saying
the words our bodies are
too tired to say

i can pretend to forget your name
i wasn't listening for two years
what scar? one you left?
foolishness, on my part
the difference is now they are
just scars, not wounds and
i have separated myself from
what you made me feel
once upon a time

open your mind up
to new possibilities
you would not be mentally able
to think up something
you could not be
if you can,
then you have proven to yourself
a power that is undeniable
yet silent

the winter cries for summer,
the summer burns for winter,
autumn and spring loiter
unknowingly in between
two b r o k e n a p a r t
lovers.

summer

to think i let anything
let alone a man
bring me down
i am strong
the daughter of nature
your shoes will never destroy me
how you batter the ground
with every step you take

remind yourself to feel
but remind yourself in a painless
and a loving way

gurpreet raulia

the bees fly around me
yearning for my legs and arms
sweet honeysuckle skin
deep honey filled eyes
dripping straight from the stars
trying to constellate me

i will never open my arms again
and welcome with a cup of tea
nor a loaf of bread
such a disguised monster
who will rid me of my sustenance

i will cleanse you
would you like some honey and lemon?
sinuses clear and
i want you to breathe
the freshest air and i want
every cell, every centimetre
of your existence to feel
rejuvenated and calm

hold the oxygen
in your lungs for a touch
longer and remember
you can breathe

the universe looks after me
better than razors and
strawberry shaving creams
it's planting flowers in my skin
watches me bloom in spring
showers me in autumn
looking after me so carefully
and i am only doing injustice
by being made to feel
as though i need to shave off her creation
when she's coming back for a reason
she is purity

i could never grasp
the idea of 'god'
because i'd never submit myself
to anyone
until i realised that 'god' is nowhere
except within me
and now i feed her
water her
i make her real
God is within me, i am my own God

our hearts evolve with the times
and like the sun reappears
once the storm has cleared
your smile will once again show
once the sadness has gone

-just a visitor

the sunsets change us
turning orange and pink
like peculiar fruits
the earth stood still for a minute
whilst nature suckled sweetly at our skin
and the crickets hummed in the softness

your gentility is a gift
you held my hand though holding
just a petal
there is goodness within your soul
within your touch
your aura holds me captive
you, the child of the suns orbs

gravity brings you down
and you crash on the rocks
before you stream so effortlessly
Canadian water, your purity
you are in your own form
you have been on a journey
and have come out so beautiful
now you come out of our taps
at home and cleanse us, daily

your voice is like sweet jazz
smooth like warm milk tea
it makes the birds outside
so happy to be alive
they sing along

the hustle and bustle of the tube
the endless 'sorry's
the endeavour to get lost in the masses
where you're nothing but a traveller,
exploring the world amongst us

you are trapped in the lapping,
washed away with the ocean
drowning in your everlasting
ups and downs and motions
but you are pure, the water on this earth
i'll gladly drink you up
because even troubled waters
can become calm once again

the hava took me in other directions
it embraced me through the whirlwinds
and set me down slowly
it promised it would not let me fall
it helped me find peace
it made my hair look alive

-hava: air, wind

gurpreet raulia

you felt like a solitary island
buoyed on the waters
i step onto it and i sink with it
but i feel warm and encased
like a bath in the winter
the hands of nature giving me her love
i feel her care for me
i am no longer afraid to drown

176

you are not my earth but you carried me
you are not my bath but you cleansed me
you are not my water but you refreshed me
you are not my pain but you hurt me
you are not my bed but you comforted me
you are not my past but you defined me
you are not my present but you gifted me
you are not my future but you will guide me

art comes in colour
colour comes through art
through my mind comes
my culture and in my art
comes my mind
my canvas is my platform
my paint is my voice
my voice box is awfully tired
but my hands will work everlong
to translate my words for me

the bees choose not to pollenate from you
they know your juices are poisoned
they fly past you feeling smug

your stories are written on your skin
i feel empowered i feel educated,
just by looking at you,
there are maps in your skin
the way to get to the wheat fields
from the house
past the tree so many of my ancestors
have circled after marriage,
walking and feeling the soft ground
beneath our skin,
covered in dust and dirt
and beautifully clean still
the truth of the land we left behind
ingrained in our bodies

dressing my hair in thick castor oil
restoring my Indian thickness
which was taken away
by colonising hands
with a pair of thinning scissors
that i don't recall asking for
i will regrow and come back
full force in my Indian glory

like moisture to cotton candy
i wipe your skin with cotton
and it melts so soon
it has never known something so soft
unlike itself

-carnival

i embrace the thickness of my hair
i have no issue in not
ripping out my grass from its roots
i feel no need to look pretty
i am pretty, 'clean'
voice of my culture
that you attempt to mute with
wax, thread, metal clips,
my darkness is my beauty

i see so much in blank spaces
i let my imagination run wild
i want yours to too

.

angel rises from the river
every time the sun glitters upon it
each wave signifying the wave
of a cherub, the smile of
the holy goodness
entering each person
who looks its way

gurpreet raulia

i stitch us back up at the seams
after i ripped us apart
i wanted to make us perfect,
patchwork can be beautiful too?

we cover our heads in our holy place
we take off our shoes
we eat our holy blessed food
we sit in ambience and we reconnect
we sit cross-legged on the floor
religion brings us to the ground
and keeps us grounded

gurpreet raulia

don't give yourself the privilege
to believe that you are
so great, so mighty,
did you think i was so impressionable
that i would not overcome you
regardless of your habit of
coming back, my door will always
be closed to you

there is a beauty in women
that i was never afraid to admit
i always embraced this way i felt
let nobody ever try to define me
it seeped into my dreams
when i was with a man
my heart humbled with the honesty
to feel exactly how it wants to feel

scoop me up like nut butter
i'll be the healthier alternative
i'll be your diet
i'm easier than the rest of them
i can never place that weight on your
shoulders
i'll keep you clean

my mother, a child
stories of hiding under trees
jumping over walls
looking after cows
the Indian soil at her feet
her family leaving her behind
in search for a new life
somehow better
India written in her blood
patience written in the mud

someone else's sheer blindness
to your worth
has no weighting
on your value
a non-materialist may not like diamonds
but that doesn't mean you're not one

put your gloves on
rub your hands
i'm quite the catch
strike the others out

hold the hands of your sisters
and wipe the tears of your brothers
be there and plait the hair of our mothers
fear not the fragile identity of our lovers
and rejoice in the education on life
that we receive from others

they teach us the poetry of the whites
in class, and it makes me feel unpoetic
as a result because
i can not replicate that, or channel that
my poetry is not that of shakespeare's
it's that of rumi's, or rupi's,
my poetry is brown, my poetry is sand
it runs through your fingers
it's written in english but my poetry
my poetry has no language but the language
of colour and the tongue
of honesty, with the world
and myself

gurpreet raulia

i feel sad that i separated myself
from my roots, from my home country.
now i feel so connected to all the people
ironically from my own endeavour
to learn
people that were lost in the battles
their days numbered and fates written
by somebody other than themselves
now they are just numbers and stories
but i will learn about them
and i will make them alive again

when i saw you had moved on
i felt so much relief
the last piece of you had finally let me
i finally knew you no longer thought
about me and i felt blessed
that a piece of me would no longer associate
with you
you never deserved for my name
to circulate in your head

you are made of two hydrogen atoms
and one oxygen
and i feel the consequences
of all your awakening properties
wash me, fill me in like an empty
periodic table,
stabilise me

you were my rough working out
and now i'm looking for the right
definitive answer

there is simply
so much equality in our
love and it is simply
all i could ever ask for
i am grateful forever
you banquish the nether
and calm our weather
if i had three wishes
you'd make a hat-trick

blessings blessings blessings
you have placed upon my head
you have turned the darkness inside out
and i am flowering once again

my bones are rejoining
my heart is rejoicing
happiness is such a strange feeling
i feel changed from within
like an outfit that i feel great in
i feel brand new

there are too many days
in your life's calendar
for you to believe that there won't be
one day, out of a possible 29,200 days,
when you'll finally realise
that you are worthy

follow the sun darling
she'll take you to beautiful places
seek the oceans and the mountains
bring yourself closer to the world
you were so lucky to be placed on

you want to be made to feel
feel good things wild things
the wildflowers dancing inside
with an iridescent beauty
you want your insomnia to be made
into sleepless nights of laughter
instead of restless hours of anxiety
you want the butterflies inside your tummy
instead of moths flying out of your crevices
you want to be made to feel
like the single most precious human
being on this planet
that's what you do to me
that's what you do to me

gurpreet raulia

you, there is goodness in your aura
you, i love your heart the water
runs so freely from it i find you
refreshing, hydrating you are
the river in the dessert
the painkiller for the headache
the coffee for the fatigue
the food for the soul,
you

you are a piece of artwork
but you are the artist
you hold the paintbrush

i would pick you
at any jewellery shop
i would adorn myself
with you, the best
decoration

you get suffocated for
who you are but
breathe darling
i'm so happy you're alive

take 30 seconds of your day
use a sandtimer if you must
just ask if they're okay
it might be all they need

i want to voice things that
awaken others
that hurt others
that love others
that make people
reflect
i want to be your voice
i want to be my own voice

lick my lips
they're coated in sugar
kiss me so gently
that the sugar doesn't leave

don't waste time missing people
who hurt you in the name of love
you need someone who will
love you kindly, respectfully,
with nurture,
and not selfishly

gurpreet raulia

7,600,000,000 people on earth
and you want to tell me
you won't find anyone
honey
you don't even have to look

conquer each day,
one at a time,
thinking nothing of
tomorrow, nor yesterday,
and make today,
your day,
everyday

don't try to outsmart your emotions
your heart is capable of so much
to limit the way it feels is injustice
and damaging to the self
instead of trapping the spiders inside you
from fear of seeing them true
let them out and free them
let go of the thunders inside of you

your smile is one hundred times
more comforting
than any words anyone has
ever used to make me feel
anything

gurpreet raulia

freshly washed hair
soaked in bubblegum glory
adorned with flowers
you, goddess, your youth
is shining through with its rays
thin but wide and i really
love you

-cleansing

your struggle is personal but
that means not that
you are alone as
the world is here with open arms
to embrace you and your essences
to complete you and nurture you
and be your umbrella in the rain
until your overcast skies become
bright once again;

muffled sounds of ambient music
fill the atmosphere whilst you're
here in my soul and my mind
but your physical being is so far away
i block out the noises, the coffee machines
and replace them with the loud reminders
of your existence and your smile
your hands holding mine so tight whilst
i tap at these keys you're here
with me in the cold room of warmth
missing your warmth, your comfort

i began telling my mother
the love i have for her
though formerly i expressed it
by the tea i would leave for her
for when she returned for work
or the plate of scrambled eggs and
pan fried toast, because that's how she likes it
but ever since she used her voice
to tell the man who attempted to send us away
that she can never leave her children
i have reminded her everyday
that i love her so dearly
with the voice that she so righteously
afforded for me

embellish me with flowers drape me with
silk sheets and dress me in yoghurt
and honey make me feel regal
love my royalty and adorn me
your queen, your love,
be my whole kingdom
i've always been the pauper

i am no longer afraid
to confront you
since you are no longer
a member of my community
you are an outsider now
and there is nothing in
my body that feels
belittled by you anymore
i have won

you help maintain my homeostasis
you keep me balanced
i feel the scales and you are
perfectly equal, there is no overpowering
i kiss your brown lips, euphoria
you kiss me with the love in your eyes

my family are the tea
my friends are the water
you are the milk
i am complete

gurpreet raulia

i can sip nectar from your lips
it drips from your fingers
it melts off your chest
i have never felt so nourished
the bees think you are their god

dandelions swimming through
the thick air, thick with lost
love stories and broken hearts
all these wishes for happiness now sitting
in my hair, is this, where
you all wanted it to go
i am decorated with the hopelessness
of all the other attempts for
dreams to come true
and now being fuelled
to right the wrongs

poetry is soul food
a hearty soup filled
with vegetables and
the bits of pasta you
love to find floating
in the liquid joy,
it's the stew made of
christmas leftovers,
poetry is nutrition
it's wholesome and
it fills in the hunger
we ache to be taken
care of for us

when the world is becoming
unaligned and the constants
are changing
recentre yourself and reconcentrate
your energies, your vibrations
into an ultimate being within
that will keep you balanced
and levelled like lady justice's scales
to keep you upright and at peace

you make my world
a better place
you know not of your powers
or the supernatural nature
of the way you make me feel
as i did not think
that there'd come a day
that someone would mow the overgrown
grass within my mind
and sow seeds for sunflowers
catching the light as i walk

remind yourself that
you are one with the stars
though you look at them in
amazement they
are shining at you they are saying
hello, it's so nice to see you again
and they shine to make sure
you can see them
they've missed you,
smile for them

i normally don't take
sugar with my tea but
here you are, my 0 calorie
sweetener. guilt free lovin'

head in the clouds, in
that gap that we found,
find yourself grounded
again and let the sun's rays
pour through and warm you

my body is a temple
don't bring your sin near me
permanent restraining order
i have sole custody
over myself

-entitlement

you think you're
buried but
really, you're planted,
now bloom baby

like orchids, sometimes
your flowers will wilt but,
embrace the process and trust in
your capabilities
like orchids you will bloom
once again

when death knocks on
my very door
i will just shut it on him
i'm not done yet

-no junk mail

shakur rose from the concrete
and i am flower without rain
having used my own blood
as my water, retracing my roots
and drawing out for the reign

that soul of yours
is so radiant but not
so much as your eyes
which tries its hardest
to hold all of that shining
within them

-'the eyes are the windows to the soul'

one day i let go of
the stress and anxiety
that came bundled up with
the relationships i yearned
to build with others and for once
i stopped and scanned the waters of
my own life and decided i
needed to create for once
a relationship with, myself
and that was the day
i saw my flowers being to bloom
the day, i finally saw growth

-hydroponics

your most important
friendship is truly
with yourself

be the artist of yourself,
paint yourself and display
yourself in the galleries
of your heart and penetrate the
galleries of others' hearts and minds. make them
feel blessed to have ever seen
such a masterpiece

people will always want what
you have and that's why
people have tried to steal
famous artwork. you are
my mona lisa. you are
mine.

remember to find God
within your being, guide
and have limitless faith
in yourself, always

let your sadness and happiness
coexist at times
there is nothing wrong with not
having joy at all times
you can patch up the soil
next to where flowers are blooming
they will go through all seasons, together
dream balance dear, dream the
balance and bring the dream
to your reality

'i had no idea you were Indian
you're so fair, i thought you were
from italy, or somewhere around there,
you're so pale for an Indian,
you're so beautiful'
to all my brown girls
out there, don't let anyone's
colourism make you feel lesser
we can be beautiful in every season
they'll continue to look for the sun
they just want us to be their spectacle
you are your own spectacle
brown girl, you are beautiful

you raise the hairs on the back
of my soft neck so far they could
fall out and they never yearn
to leave as they've refused to be pulled
by any wax or thread
but you're so close

we may live one life
but we can have so many
lives, you can always reform
you can always start again
gaining enough points to be
satisfied by the end
one falter isn't the end
it's the beginning of a new journey

you know exactly
what a woman needs to hear
when she doesn't know it herself
and that is the most
underappreciated feature on the
smartphone that is you
you are like a guru in the shape
of a lover, not someone
who takes advantage of our
confusion, but helps us
and gives us space, and proves
us that there's goodness out there

-the good men

you are like the Vancouver night
sky to me, you are not an
object, you are a feeling i just
can't describe

i couldn't care less if you miss me
i am eternally grateful
counting myself lucky
for my lucky escape

drive him wild, flower
find joy in the power struggle

she should only have you
crying about
how happy she makes you
in the day, in the night,
in the life we can't exchange
or relive, what are sad tears
worth compared to the
grander scheme of the existence
of our own partners, families, friends,
us

as a woman i will
stand behind a woman so much so
that i will not feel afraid
to tell them when they
are wrong, this is the ultimate
level of respect

because of you i now have hope
of being someone better
there is a newfound maturity
i believe i need
this is not about the you being
the right person
at the wrong time
this is about being me
the wrong person at
the right time,
to recognise myself,
i must change myself,
and be the better person
the better person
because you are the
best person, for me

in the name of art,
i love everything in your essence,
you are my muse.

i fall into this galaxy
swimming endlessly in purple and
blue and feeling red and pink
drowning in flesh within your
sheets or mind, too high to recall,
too low to forget so let's
play our favourite playlist
or our favourite frank ocean album
and lose ourselves in our
own abyss again, together;

breathe in power
breathe out inspiration
wake up and love
sleep in happiness
live in peace
you are all that matters

the universe is so lucky
to see us grow in its game
creating sweet symphonies
inspiring art to die
in the most beautiful way
sweet caramel guitar strums
sweet honey in poetic lines
rid of sickliness
recovering and inventing new ambition
the arched back of the lover
the gleaming smile of the friend
the unconditional love of the mother
the caresses of the earth
letting us bloom, endlessly